Discover Self Redemption

Victoria Terrana

BookLeaf Publishing

Presentation by *BookLeaf Publishing*

Web: www.bookleafpub.com

E-mail: info@bookleafpub.com

ISBN : 9789357699563

First edition 2022

PREFACE

Topics in this book include the importance of worth, the depth and value in how you love, solitude, self contentment, the effects of insecurity, how insecurity can put you in a toxic relationship, leaving behind an ex partner, what a healthy partner looks like, dealing with loss, making words become reality, self esteem, God's love, choosing love and morality over hate, and the importance of expressing God's love.

Worthwhile Worth●❤

Nobody can take your worth away,
No matter what one may do or say.
They cannot ruin your day.
Your worth is not worth fighting for,
Let them wait at your door.
Do not let them push you to the floor.

Remember you are enough.
Within your soul you are more than tough.
Some may appreciate your beauty.
But some may step right on you with no shame and no remorse.
But remember it is their loss.

You can be strong with the ones who love you,
You don't need to wait for those who won't wait for you.
There's no time for waiting for those who are behind you.
Their souls cannot seem to find you.

They are swimming in the poison of jealousy and hate,
They are not worth the wait.
Their souls are so behind,
They cannot understand why you are kind.

Keep persistent.
Keep strong.
Walk ahead.
You won't be stuck for long.
Soon moving on won't seem so wrong.
Appreciate that rare beauty in your soul,
And keep climbing towards your goal.

The Vision of Insecurity

Because of my insecurity,
I constantly needed surety.
Surety that he would always be there,
That he would always care,
That we would always be a pair.

But my vision must be changed.
My priorities must be rearranged.
My insecurity tells me he's a good fit,
While his character is not good one bit.
My "surety" says he's the one,
While there was nothing special he has done.

My lonliness says he's good for me,
Because my lonliness cannot see.
All she knows is comfort in not being alone,
But now it's time that I let her moan.

She needs to learn solitude,
She cannot let others affect her mood.
She needs to let others be rude,
She needs to taste her soul's own food.

My lonliness needs to die,
And soon my solitude will no longer rely on a guy.

My lonliness may still cry,
But my solitude will easily say goodbye.
And she will know exactly why.

My solitude will have no problem leaving.
My lonliness may still be grieving,
But my solitude will stop believing.
She no longer believes insecurity's lies.
And now she is firm in her goodbyes.

When Pride was Tried

You disabled me,
You did not let me be.
You said I cannot,
So my soul began to rot.

I wanted to try,
But I believed your lie.
I wanted to begin,
But I let your pride win.
I gave into sin.

You said I could not drive,
I was not allowed to live alive.
You made me ask for a ride.
I needed to follow your guide.

You said it was safe for me to confide,
There was no need for me to hide.
I listened to the voice of your pride.

I was on your side.
I leaned on you during a tide.
Yet your arms would not open up wide.
Then I realized you had lied.
That was the day my love for you had died.

Your Beautiful Love❤

Don't let your beauty pass you by,
Don't let how people treat you make you cry.
Your beauty is found in your love and care.
That is why your beauty is so rare.

Appreciate your beauty without expecting
anything from others.
Yet continue to love them as sisters and brothers.

You don't need their approval to know your
worth,
You don't need their respect to know you're
worthy of love.

But respect yourself enough to know,
That distance from some may help you grow.
Approve yourself enough to understand,
Your worth is not found in lending a hand.

Love and care for those whose love and care is
returned.
Your love and care must be earned,
It has no right to be burned.
This is the most important lesson you have
learned.

Living "Lonely"⚫⬛

Lonliness may still exist,
But he can longer tie your wrists.
No matter how much he insists,
You continue to resist.

You fell in love with your being,
You love the new way you're seeing.
This is so much more freeing.

Lonliness can no longer tie you down,
He can no longer make you frown.
Lonliness no longer makes you settle for less,
You are no longer swayed by one trying to impress.

Now you know that you are enough,
And alone you are more than tough.
Even when times get rough,
You can stay strong,
Because Love is now the melody to your song.

You are still alone,
But you no longer groan.
Lonliness did not leave,
But he is no longer the one you believe.

Now you can start living,
And receive the love you kept giving.
Now that you put aside his lies,
You can let God's love arise.

Choose Love

Oh what joy Love is bringing!
Hear the sound of your heart singing.
You pulled out dead weeds,
And decided to plant new seeds.

There is no room for one weed to remain,
There is only one thing your field can contain-
The seeds that will yield grain.

Now look at the bountiful grains of wheat!
Hear the sweet sound of your heart beat,
Rest in her embrace; take a seat.

You plowed the field,
Now look at all you were able to yield!
You nourished the soil.
You remained loyal.
You gathered the harvest before it could spoil.

Be glad and rejoice!
You listened to Love's voice.
You made the right choice.
Now Love is here to greet you.
Because greed could not defeat you.

God's Love is Yours

I will love you with all my heart,
I will go out of my way to make sure you are safe.
I want you to be comfortable.
There is nothing I want more than you to be in good health.

Your joy is my joy.
Your heart is my heart.
Your safety is my safety.
Your peace is my peace.
Your well being is my well being.

What does my joy mean to you?
Does my heart have any meaning?
Do you worry about my safety?
Does my peace matter?
Does my well being have an impact?

My life may not be important to you.
My existence may have no impact on you.
My well being may not matter at all to you.

But do you know what is important?
Do you know what does matter?
You know what does have an impact?

The love I am able to give,
The love I can give to someone who has no love to give,
The love I am filled with when nobody was willing to pour that love in me.

Where did this love come from?
How is it so bountiful?
How does it keep seeping through a soul that used to be so empty?
What filled my soul when nobody really helped?

My Lord filled me up.
He fills me up every day.
People can put me down.
They can make me feel like I am worthless.
But when I remember my Lord,
When I remember how much I am truly loved,
When I remember I am not alone no matter how physically lonely I may feel,
I am filled up with the love of my Lord once again.

He never fails to fill me up.
He never fails to pick my up when I fall.
He wants me to keep on going.
He wants me to keep spreading that love He gives me.

He knows I can do it because He created me to do it.

Therefore, I will keep on going.
I will accept my Lord's love,
I will keep on spreading that love,
That out of this world love,
The kind of love I may never get from a human,
But the kind of love I receive every day from my gracious God.

Make your Love Greater than your Loss❤

My mind knows he's gone,
But my heart doesn't believe it.
She still thinks he's coming back.
My mind thinks this is whack.

How long will my heart be in denial?
Soon my mind will put her on trial.
Will she be able to handle the truth?
Will she be okay that the truth isn't the truth she wants?

Surely my heart will fight with my mind for a while,
But who will be stronger?
Who will win the war?
Who will be the one to leave at the door?
Who will surrender?
Who will be the last standing member?

My heart wants what will make her feel full,
But my mind doesn't want to hear the bull.
My heart wants to be filled with hope.
But my mind calls me a dope.
My heart is just thinking these things to cope,
Yet my mind keeps telling me what's true.

And this makes my heart feel blue.
She wish she never had this loss.
She can't seem to handle the costs.

The heart may be moving slow,
The mind may make her feel low,
But the heart is powerful in her love,
She may not believe her man is gone,
She may hold onto a false hope,
But she will believe the mind when she is ready.
In the meantime, she will remain steady.

My heart will never give up on her love for this dead man,
No matter how long he is gone, she will never forget him,
She will never fall short of her love for him,
Although he is no longer here to hug her,
She will love him with the love of a mother,
She will continue to cradle him in her soul,
She will caresses him with her gentle hand.

The mind may never understand,
Because he is not in her land.
The heart's land is filled with unending affection,
She doesn't want the mind's correction.
The mind may believe what is true,

But he doesn't know what the heart always knew.

Love and affection is always in her being,
Their fruits have always been freeing,
Eyes of love is how she was always seeing.
She will forever love the one who passed,
She wishes his life didn't go fast,
But she knows that regardless of time or weather.
In her heart, he will last forever.

Don't Ask Me Why

Now is my time to say goodbye.
Don't ask me why.
I am now restoring my strength.
Don't ask me where I went.

Having me around was convenient.
Yet you weren't lenient.
For so long,
You told me I was wrong.
You didn't let me be strong.

My emotions,
Were "commotions".
My every opinion,
Did not have "dominion".
When I had a need,
It was interpreted as "greed".

Finally, I knew I had to leave.
This is something I never wanted to believe.
But now, I am able to breathe.
I am finally able to receive.
Receive the love that I kept giving.
The love that kept forgiving.

Does Love Have a Dialect?

Does love have a dialect?
Is this something I should inspect?
Because I don't understand.
How can different love live in the same land?

Love has a language barrier.
One love may not be able to hear another.
No matter how much one tries.
The other love continually defies.

His love was silence,
My love was communication.
His love was short responses.
My love was thoughtful words.

His love required blind obedience.
My love required an informed decision.
His love required my approval.
My love was willing to accept the most brutal.

His love was his way.
My love was understanding.
His love was his convenience.
My love went out of her way.

His love was his ego.

My love was my heart.
His ego was loyal to his reputation.
My heart was loyal to his heart.

Different love will always fight.
Each will claim to be right.
Because each had different sight,
There is no common ground on which they can unite.

Greed Will Not Succeed

Greed was never kind,
He wanted dominion over my mind.
He wanted me to believe he was one with whom
I could confide.
But he was really just filled with pride.
He was never actually on my side.

He did what he could,
To convince me he was good.
To make sure I would stay.
To make sure he got his way.

When he got my trust,
He became friends with lust.

I never loved him,
He took advantage of my love.
I was never loved by him.
He took advantage of my trust.

He claimed he would treat me good.
Words were his favorite trick.
He was a successful dick.
For a while, his words did stick.

Until one day,

I found my way.
My way out of this mess,
Of this asshole trying to impress.

I said this is enough,
I finally became tough.
For too long, he made my life rough.

I said goodbye,
Without an explanation why.
Because he simply was not my guy.

When I Loved Hate

For a while I loved hate,
I thought he was my fate.
He was the only one I wanted to date.

I loved loving hate,
He didn't care about me,
But I enjoyed caring about him.

One day, I realized I couldn't love him much longer,
Because he was not making me stronger.
The more love I shared,
The less he cared.
He knew I wouldn't mind,
So he took advantage of me being kind.

I had no limits in giving,
And he had no limits in taking.
He never loved me.
He loved how I loved him.
He never cared about me.
He cared about how I cared about him.

Now it is time that I have no limits in giving to myself.
No limits in saying no to another.

No limits in loving myself.

No limits in loving true love.
No limits in staying away from hate.
He is no longer the one I date.
Because I will not let him be my fate.

Bringing Action Verbs to Life

Words may sound promising and bright,
But only actions will bring them to light.
If only words would go on strike,
So that actions can go on the hike.
Life would make so much more sense.
Without having words put you in suspense.

Make actions a part of your face,
May words no longer have a place.
In your heart, there is no more space.
Words will not win the race.

Only actions will help you move up more and
more,
Words will leave you waiting at the door.
Words will bring you to the floor,
They will keep asking you to pour.
They will start a war.

But they cannot withstand an action's roar.
They will be in awe at how high actions soar.
There is no one else you would rather adore.
Now it's time to leave words at the door,
And make actions your heart's core.

Let His "Love" Die

It is better to be alone,
Than to be in a relationship and groan.
If you are not content,
You don't need to resent.
But you need more than space,
You need to restore joy to your face.

Your soul feels beat,
But soon you will get back on your feet.
As you walk away,
You may feel a bit grey.
Comfort will influence you to stay.
But remember you are walking the right way.

You are leaving what caused you ache,
For your "lover's" sake.
Your peace is most vital.
Don't make pain your idol.
You are more precious than you can ever see.
So live the way God made you to be.

Greed may not say his goodbyes,
Because you are the one on which he relies.
He lives with ill-intent.
He is quick to resent.
Yet, he "loves" when he wants you back.

He is a never-ending hack.

As you let his plees pass by,
He will continue to sigh.
But remember how he let you cry.
He was not your guy.
But you're still waiting for his "love" to die.

Your Heart is the Best Part❤

I forgot my soul was dead,
Because my mind forgot she was alone,
He forgot she was worthless,
He forgot about her lost love.

Then my soul came back to life.
She remembered she had her own company,
She gave herself her worth,
She found love inside of her.

I may have lost public approval,
I may have lost people I used to be "close to",
But do you know whose approval I never lost?
Do you know who's closeness will never fade away?

I will never lose my heart.
I will never lose her friendship.
I was never "wrong",
I was never "inadequate",
I was never "unlovable".
I was exactly what my mind told me I was.
My mind told me to believe these things,
He told me to cry because they were true.
He told me there was nothing I can do.

Yet, my heart helped me to forget to cry,
And most importantly, she told me why.
She helped me to realize that the mind is a liar.
She told me to throw his lies in the fire.

She restored my soul when she died.
She comforted me when I cried.
She gave me peace in my own company,
She reminded me of my worth,
She told me about the love I was made of from birth.

I don't like my mind,
But I let him talk as long as he needed,
Yet, his advice is no longer heeded.
I now listen to my best friend, my heart.
She has took care of me from the start.
Her love is unending,
And I know she is not pretending.

No matter how many times my soul dies,
No matter how many times she cries,
The peace in my heart will always rise.
Her love will take away the mind's lies.

Love♥ or Comfort?●

I was here to help you heal,
There was no need for you to conceal.
But you were not here for me,
So we are not meant to be.

I was in love with you,
Always concerned about your days.
But you were just comfortable with me,
Simply used to my ways.

When I was there to care,
You were filled with joy.
Yet, when my pain was too much to bear,
You said, "Oh boy."

In order for me to heal,
You wanted me to conceal.
I tried my best,
Being alone in my distress.

I was your joy,
But I soon became your toy.
You were an important part of my day,
Until you started to play.

Date "The One"

Date the one who will wait.
Date the one who loves what is right and just.
The one who will not give into lust.
Date the one who loved God first,
The one who will love you at your worst.

Date the one who will love what is above more than what is here.
Date the one who will not give into fear.
The one who will always hold you dear.

Date the one who won't see you as less,
Just because of your mess.
Date the one who will bring out your best,
The one who will be your place of rest.

Date the one who encourage your every dream,
The one one who make you face beam.
Date the one whose presence makes you smile.
The one who is willing to go the extra mile.

Date the one whose love is more than words he could say,
Date the one whose love is actions that brighten your day.

Date the one whose love does not depend on his mood,
The one who will not be rude.

Date the one who doesn't need to be told how to love you,
The one who knows what he must do.
Date the one whose love will not delay,
The one whose love is always here to stay.

A Ride that Cannot Drive

I got a ride,
But he doesn't know how to drive.
He picked me up,
But he isn't taking me anywhere.
He is mine,
But am I his?

My heart doesn't know what my mind is telling me.
My heart can't give up,
But my mind keeps telling me to.
The heart moves slower than the mind,
The mind can get over anything,
But the heart needs time.

Needs time to unlove who she loved for so long,
Who she loved so dearly.
Whom she loved more than the person loved her.
She loved him more than the mind could understand,

The mind knew what was true.
Knew he could not drive.
Knew he could not handle your heart.
Knew he could never understand the purpose of your heart's depth.

Knew he could not ever appreciate it to it's fullest.
Knew that he could never choose you the way you choose him,

Knew the heart will always love him,
But will soon have to listen to the mind.
Soon the heart will have no choice.
The heart will be exhausted of all it's efforts.
The heart will need to find someone who can drive.

Love is Not a Debate 🖤

No matter how people treat you,
Never let hate defeat you.
You are stronger than the bullies around you.
You can embody the love that found you.
You can overcome the hate that may surround you.

You are greater than the violence inside your mind.
You can have a lasting peace that will make you kind.
Love is the most beautiful thing you will find.
Now is the time to leave hate behind.

You are your best remedy.
Only you can make yourself see.
People can try to assist,
But you may still resist.

Someone's assistance may not help you no matter their good will,
Their efforts will not always fill.
You can't look for a remedy on a shelf.
Only you have the power to fill yourself.

You are enough no matter how different you are,

No matter how hard it gets you can still raise
your bar.
Culture will try to blur your moral sense.
Make you think you should be in suspense.

But morality never changed.
People's priorities were just rearranged.
They will continue to try to justify the wrong,
But they won't get away with it for long.

What is wrong can never become right,
Justice will always win the fight.
How is morality open for discussion?
Morality is not a debate.
There is only one way love can be our fate.

Are you willing to enter Love's gate?
Will you rid yourself of culture's hate?
Or will you let it win the debate?
How much longer will you wait?

Your Unwavering Worth🌚💜🔥

When your mind begins to wander,
Your worth and value is something you shall ponder.
There is nothing more noble and right,
Than to see your beauty and readjust your sight.

You are more valuable than all of creation,
You are worth more than a yearly vacation.
There is nothing more necessary in God's eyes,
Than for you to look in the mirror and see His prize.

Now is the time your insecurity dies.
And you become wise,
There is nothing about you to correct.
There is not one feature to inspect.

The worth and value that lies in you,
Does not depend on what you say or do.
Do not fight for your worth,
You already acquired it from birth.

The worth and value that lies in you,
Does not depend on the way one may treat you.
No matter how many times you feel defeated,
No matter how many times you are not greeted,

No matter how many expectations people could not meet,
And how many times your soul feels beat,
Your worth and beauty has been shining just as bright,
Has been the same value despite others' acts of spite.

Your worth is not worth fighting for,
If people cannot see the beauty in your core,
Leave them waiting outside your door.
Do not let them push you to the floor.

They will keep asking for more,
Yet they will not be willing to pour.
There is no need to start a war,
But make your worth the treasure you most adore.

Love's Creator

You are by yourself with your Lord,
You are alone, but with Him.
You are in a space,
With the creator of the human race.

Your God is here,
Being alone is nothing to fear.
Your Lord is enough,
Even when times get rough,
Remember you are more than tough.

Be yourself with confidence,
Allow your soul to radiate each room,
And other hearts will begin to bloom.
Stand up straight,
Love is your fate.

God, You are not lacking,
Your skills aren't slacking.
You give life to everything that's dying,
You cheer faces that were once crying.

Oh God, love is not something You need,
It's something You precede.
You created it.
But, there were times we hated it.

Because love required loss,
We couldn't handle the cost.

But we have learned to rise above,
And be an expression of your love.
You gave us company when we were alone,
You showed us our strength when we wanted to groan.

We can now stand taller than a tower.
Because You shared your superpower,
It makes us more beautiful than a flower,
It makes us sweet towards those who are sour.
We are here because of who You are,
And because of You, we will go far.

www.ingramcontent.com/pod-product-compliance
Lightning Source LLC
Chambersburg PA
CBHW051746130826
49812CB00033B/1021
9789357699563